HOW TO BUILD AND DEVELOP A MAIL ORDER BUSINESS

AND MARKET IT THROUGH THE INTENET

Xiang-Wen Ma

May, 1998   San Diego, CA USA

Table of Contents

Executive Summary

The Purpose of the Plan

The following is Fortune Star International, Inc.'s research study and business plan on how to start up a mail order business and how to operate it successfully and efficiently. It will help our company to set our goals and objectives and provide a basis for evaluating and controlling our business. It is our first attempt of strategic planning. It will serve as a guidance and direction for FSI Inc. to start the business. The plan will be updated and improved periodically to reflect the changes and actual circumstances once the business gets started.

The Concept

Fortune Star International Inc. is going to be a home-based mail order business selling gift items mainly through Internet advertising and have the products delivered to the homes across the whole United States. The concept of Fortune Star International is to offer refreshing and creative gift products not readily to find at the stores and have them delivered right to the homes of customers. It offers not only the convenience of shopping but also the opportunity to get unique gift ideas at a very reasonable price. Currently in the United States, more and more people are doing mail order business at their home. In fact, mail order business has become one of the most popular money making opportunities for people who want to own their own business. People are doing it full time or on a part-time basis. According to the estimation on the Internet, for every two seconds, there are 800 mail order businesses coming into existence today which makes mail order one of the fastest growing segments in direct marketing. The driving force behind mail order business rush is the fact that it offers people a great opportunity to make money at the convenience of their home without big financial commitment to get started and the fact that more and more people are doing their shopping needs via mail order delivery.

Offering products at a reasonable price to interested customers through the mail is not a new concept. Mail order's roots can be traced back more than 100 years ago. Why is mail order growing? For one reason, it's much easier than buying retail. With mail order, customers don't have to experience fighting for parking spaces, swollen feet from standing in line, or pushy sales clerks. For these reasons, shopping via mail order is truly a painless experience. Mail order also offers larger amount of selections than retail stores.

Today, with the rapid growth of the information age, people are relying more and more on the telecommunication to get everything done. From getting information for their research to buying gifts for their loved ones. Based on our research findings, today, there are more than 60 million people in America who are connected with Internet. This offers us a tremendous opportunity to set up a mail-order business with the aid of Web promotion to offer the products people always want to buy. This is how the original idea of Fortune Star International came from.

Market Analysis

Based on the market research we conducted, there is a great demand for gift items in American market such as dolls, toys, ornaments, artistic appliances, handicrafts, fine porcelain works and so on. People need those products for any occasions such as birthdays, weddings, anniversaries, all different holidays, friends and family reunions, and all kinds of celebrations and socials. Fortune Star International will be able to fill people's need for gift products by offering creatively and beautifully designed crafts and art works made in the Orient. Even though our market seems very large, our target market segment will be female homeowners married with Children. They are the ones who are most likely to purchase gift items numerous times a year for their families, their children, their relatives, their friends, their colleagues and bosses, and for themselves at different occasions. Through market research and test, we are sure that our products are going to fill the market need. Yet, in order to be successful in serving this segment, Fortune Star's business strategy will be focused on providing customers with unique, special, creative, and good quality gift products at very competitive prices. Lower prices and discount prices will be one of the most important elements to be successful in the female market.

The Company

Fortune Star International, Inc. is going to be founded in the form of a corporation to conduct mail order business. Its main products will be gift items which are imported from the Far East. The company is owned by Mr. Gordon and co-owned by Ms. Helen who both have rich experience in business management and international trade. The company has great advantages in providing U.S. market with unique and affordable gift items which are in great demand in today's market. Competitive prices, good quality, creative design and reliable customer services will be its key to success.

Marketing and Sales Activities

Our marketing strategy will be focused on advertising in the cybermall and major mail order catalogs to get our products recognized to the public. Marketing on the Internet is effective and cost less and it reaches millions of people. We offer seasonal and discount prices on a regular basis to attract customers and we will offer quick delivery and money back guarantee to our customers. For returning customers we will have nice little gift to show our appreciation. We will have product of the month on a regular basis just to offer something new and to fit the traditional holidays. In general, our marketing and sales strategy is to achieve sales growth on a monthly basis by effective advertising and reliable customer services.

The Financial Data

The start-up cost is around $12,000.00. They are going to be spending mainly on purchasing merchandise supply and on advertising. The business will be in operation in the summer of 1998. The prospective sales in 1999 are about $84,000 and in the year 2000 it will be around 96,000. The annual growth rate is expected to be 10 to 15 percent for the first three to four year. It will increase into a minimum of 30% after the initial several years. The objective of Fortune Star International Inc. is to grow into a wholesale and drop shipping center for mail order dealers in five years and reach its projected annual sales goal of over one million dollars within ten year.

CHAPTER I:

Market Analysis

Industry Description and Outlook

What is mail order then? According to Martin Barrier, Henry Hoke Jr., and Robert Stone, three well-known experts in the mail order field, mail order is "a Method of Selling, which relies on direct response advertising alone, to effect a measurable response and/or transaction by mail, telephone, or other interactive medium," and direct response advertising as "that which effects a measurable response and/or transaction at any location."

Traditionally, mail order is promoted through advertising in the newspaper, TV, direct mailing, catalogs. The cost of marketing through those methods can be very expensive, and lot of times people are discouraged by the advertising cost of mail order so even though they really wanted to start a mail order business, they tend to procrastinate it and wait and wait and nothing really happened. Luckily we are entering into a fast-growing information age and more and more business today are turning into Internet for marketing their products. The same is also true with mail order business. Cyber marketing will both add to and subtract from traditional forms of marketing. It will add more interactivity. But it will subtract costs. It will add more customer choices. But it will remove marketing's dependence on paper. It will add more "information value" to products and services. But it will take away barriers to starting a business or extending a business into international markets. [2]

Because mail order is not merely a business but a method of doing business, the market is wide and varied. Virtually any product with a specialized market position is a potential mail order candidate. Whether it is a magazine sold via 800 numbers on cable, or costume jewelry to a kitchen-table entrepreneur-turned-millionaire, a market is being targeted and successfully

tapped.

The mail order industry has been the scene of tremendous growth and exciting change

over the last few years. More than half the U.S. adult population ordered merchandise by mail

or phone in 1992. According to the WEFA Group, an economic research and forecasting firm,

catalog sales grew from $51.5 billion in 1992 to over $75 billion in 1996. As far as direct

marketing in general is concerned (which includes not only catalog sales, but also sales from

the Web site, commercials, infomercials, and home shopping networks), WEFA estimated the

industry generated more than $450 billion in total sales in 1996. There is an average of 20%

increase in mail order sales in the near future. The survey research firm Deloitte & Touché

reported that most catalog shoppers are female, married, college-educated homeowners in a

dual-income, three-to-four person household with annual family income between $30,000-

490,000. Representing over 60 percent of the total buying public in the United States.[3]

Along with tremendous growth in the mail order field over the past few decades, it

entails selling by mail either through:

1. Mailing out circulars, brochures, sales letters, flyers, catalogs, and/or other advertising

literature or

2. Using newspapers, magazines, radio, television, and/or other media to bring in orders or

inquires.

Targeting Market Segments

Market segmentation can help us locate and separate potentially profitable segments, or groups,

from among the total consumer population. If the selling efforts are to be directed at business,

industry, and other kinds of organizations, from among their entire populations. We must look for specific types of people or organizations toward whom or which to aim our sale efforts. Because they share one or more characteristics in common, they may indicate an interest in or the ability to pay for the kinds of products/services we'll be selling; they may be likely prospects for us. By concentrating on such segments of the population, you won't be scattering your advertising dollars like buckshot to the wind. [4]

In order to succeed in the mail order business, we must know exactly who our customers are. This means that we first need to target selected groups of prospects, consumers, or organizations, and then study those potential buyers in depth. Learn all we can about them; get to understand them fully; find out their needs and wants as well as their budget. Only after we have done considerable homework should we set out to prepare the right combinations of merchandise, pricing strategy, offers, advertisements, and the like to sell them with comparative ease.

According to Burstiner Irving we need to know the people we plan to sell to not only as individuals but also as members of groups. To accomplish the first objective, we'll need a thorough grounding in human psychology; for the second, a firm grasp of the fundamentals of social psychology is essential. That's because many factors influence the ways we behave. We're affected by both inborn traits and acquired characteristics, by our environment as well as by what we have inherited. To market goods and services successfully, we must know why - and how - people come to buy what they buy. We need to become familiar with those factors that influence purchasing behavior. [5] Many hundreds of investigations into the buying behavior of the American public have led to the accumulation of a sizable body of useful knowledge known as *consumer behavior* [6]

1). Distinguishing characteristics of our target markets

Fortune Star International's primary target will be middle class college-educated married women with children. They are home owners and their family average income will be over $40,000 a year. They represent about 60 percent of the total buying power in the U.S. This group of customers has the financial ability to purchase gift items on a regular basis yet spend their money within a budget. They are frequent catalog and mail order shoppers for three main reasons: first, as a homemaker with children and housework or as a working professional with daily work schedule, either way, they feel they are always short of time. Mail order saves them the trips of shopping around. Second, they want something special, unconventional, and creative when they do their gift shopping. Mail order offers them the opportunity to get something unusual. Third, mail order products are usually offered at lower prices than that in the department stores. For these reasons above, mail order shopping offers them a tempting appeal. Since the primary decision makers and influencers of our products will be female who are wives, daughters, mothers and they are the ones who are usually responsible for household shopping duties, we have to know their shopping behaviors and attitudes. They usually like colorful, creative, and decorative items with a lot attention to details. They like things that are elegant and beautiful. If they are the buyers instead of the receivers, they don't want to spend a lot of money on gift items. They tend to compare prices before making final decisions and they rush to sales and discounts.

Based on the above characteristics of our target market, Fortune Star International's business strategy is "small profits but quick turnover". Once customers think they got a good deal, they will come back to get more since good deals are hard to find these days. We are able to do that by getting our supplies directly from the manufacturers. We still make a reasonable profit on each product yet our goal is to satisfy the customers with what they want at a very competitive price on the market. Our products have to have lower prices, creative characters and have to have a quick delivery service in order to penetrate the market. By marketing products through the shopping malls on the Internet, FSI Inc.'s products can reach a large group of customers in an expanded geographic area. We also offer wholesale and distribution prices to retailers with larger quantity of order through our Internet web site. Our products will attract customers because of the creative and new ideas, the competitive prices and our reliable customer services. During the holiday shopping seasons, we will have sale and promotional prices for different items.

2). Primary target market size

As mentioned earlier, our primary marketing and advertising will be done through the cyberspace which will bring our product information to everyone who has access to the Internet. Our geographic market will be within the United States. Our prospective customers will be married women and men as well at the age group of 25-65, with total family income over $40,000. Theoretically, our target market is fairly large since mail order is done by mail and it doesn't require the customers physically going to the stores. This is actually one of the most attractive advantages of a mail order business. We ship products to anywhere within the U.S. We will try to meet our goal of an annual 15% to 20% market growth starting from the second year of our operation.

3). Purchasing cycle of potential customers

Research done by American Marketing Association indicates that people buy gift items 50% more during holiday times such as Christmas, Thanksgiving, Valentine's Day, Easter's, Mother's Day and etc. In order to boost sales during the non-holiday seasons, we will launch different products toward the need of sending gifts in our daily life such as to loved ones, friends, relatives, colleagues and etc. We will have products focused on different occasions such as birthdays, anniversaries, graduations, congratulation of new babies, weddings, and etc. Those need-based products are very suitable as gifts for the particular occasions. We will remind our customers in our advertising by promoting our products with different categories. We will also have some very neutral gift items just for the customers to choose for any need they have. In this way, we can avoid only seasonal sales but rather a regular year-around business.

Market Test Results

Actually we're encouraged by individual customers who bought our products at different fairs and trade shows we went in the past. In order to find out whether our products will be accepted by the market with the prices we set, we have regularly participated different trade shows and fairs. To our delightment, they were well received. Buyers all enjoyed our products very much and many of them returned back to purchase more. They were satisfied with our prices and the quality and uniqueness of our products. They frequently asked us when we are going to have our own shop. That's how we got the idea of selling gift products through the mail order business. We've also done a great deal of market test during the past year. We brought samples and pictures of our products with our wholesale and retail prices to a variety of retailers and wholesaler located in San Diego, Los Angeles as well as other parts of California. They all reacted very excited with our products. Some of them would like to order immediately. Since we didn't have a business set up yet and we only had very small amount of sample products, we were not able to fill their orders. But the market test proved to us that our products have a market and we are going to have great amount of buyers for our products. We also found out that customers feel very comfortable to buy our products at the price around $30 dollars. We concluded that we are going to price most of our products with this price range and we are still going to be able to make a profit. We are able to achieve that since we are able to order our products from the Far East suppliers at very competitive prices, besides that we are promoting our business through mail order which will eliminate the heavy cost of renting a space and hiring employees to maintain the store. This way we will be able to pass on the saving to our customers and help build our business from the ground. The major expenditure of our capital will be towards supplies and marketing.

Lead Times

Based on the fact that mail order business has a certain kind of risk of receiving fraud checks and end up in a financial loss. We will have to ask the potential customers to send the checks first and once we receive the checks we will go ahead and clear them first in the bank. Once the checks are clear, we will send the products to them right away. According to our interviews with people who have been in mail order business before, it will take about 2-3 weeks for the customers to receive the products they ordered from the time they sent the checks.

Competition

1. *Identification*

There are mainly three types of competitors we will face, they are:

a. Catalog Mail Order Companies

According to the research done by American Entrepreneur Association, there are currently over 300,000 catalogs in circulation, specializing in just about anything. [7] Those in the gift catalog mail order business should be considered the first group of competitors to our company. To name a few mail order business leaders in our field such as The Mellinger Co. and SMC (Special Merchandise Co.), they whole-sale their merchandise to the individual mail order dealers and they have thousands of mail order distributors under them. Their products running from snow balls to clocks all fall into the category of gift items. All the distributors of their products who conduct their business through mail order are in one way or another become our competitors. Other mail order businesses such as Harriet Carter which sells distinctive gift items through catalogs are all our major competitors.

b. Direct Marketers

Not only should we look to catalog competitors, but also to other direct marketers that use television, radio, periodicals, sales letter, and telemarketing to advertise. Examples like those dealers who advertise their gift products through Sunday coupon publications and deliver their ads to every family in the U.S. They may cover our market more expansively and with greater response rates. If they do, that may be a sign to shift our advertising medium to become more competitive.

c. Department Stores & Local Gift Shops

Even department stores and retail shops like Hallmarks, K-mart, Target, J-C Penny provide some main competition, although the format of the shopping experience is quite different. Some people feel more comfortable seeing and holding it in their hands first and check the details before actually buying the product. Those chain stores have a great variety of gift and crafts items to choose from and they are also well-known for their brand names, their good customer service and return policies. The local specialty stores have the advantage of carrying specialty and hard to find gift items in addition to the similar items offered by the department stores. In addition to the existing mail order businesses that sell gift products through catalogs, new mail order business offering similar products are coming into the market one after another. They should all be our competitors now or in the future. We also have to take consideration of those vendors at all different fairs or trade shows who sell similar products to the public. They also indirectly become our competitors.

2. *Strengths*

The biggest strength we possess but 90 percent of the mail order business and other local gift shops and vendors do not have is that we buy our products directly through the manufacturers in China. We've already established the business relations and trust with them which enable us to get the factory prices through them and ship the products directly to us. We are not like most of other small retail stores and mail order dealers who get their supply through wholesalers or distributors who already charged them for their benefits. Competitive prices thus become our strongest strength. Our second strength which is also one of the biggest advantages over others is that we are able to get the newest trendy products which are in great market demand immediately from the suppliers and we are also capable of giving feed backs to the manufacturers about what will sell and what is in demand based on our market research here so they will be able to make those kind of products for us if they are not available. So we are standing at a very favorable position in this kind of business. The third most important strength we have is

Our ability to satisfy customer needs. The majority of our products are not readily available in department stores and retail shops. They all have certain uniqueness in their designs, functions, and appearance. Some of them will offer thousands of years of oriental culture in them. They are good for collections and have long -lasting values. In addition to the above three most strong strengths we have related with our products. Our mail order will offer guaranteed quality and 30 days return policies. Our goal is to make our customers happy. We truly believe that excellent customer service is the first and also the most important guarantee for returning business.

3. *Weaknesses*

The main weakness we are currently experiencing is being a new start-up business which has some unfavorable barriers for us to obtain the volume of customers and generate enough capital for us to get more supplies. We are basically unknown to our market and has not established our track record yet. Our business is a home-based one and we don't have a big name or famous brand as our back up. The products are not famous branded products which are so familiar to the American market such as Hallmarks. So the first year in business we have to spend heavily to market our products and let us known by our customers. Before we reach the certain level of gross revenue, our business will be moderate which will limit our purchasing power. As the beginner in the mail order business, we still have a lot to learn along the way and we are short of experience in this field. Our financial resource is also limited. Nevertheless, with the right products, through effective management and marketing, we're confident that we will become very successful eventually.

According to Perry Wilbur in his book Money in Your Mailbox, there are 10 ways to beat the competition. [8] The following twenty ways will be Fortune Star Inc.'s guideline to beat the competition:

1). **Produce a superior product.** The most specific ways for our business to rise above our competition is to go back to the drawing board and come up with high quality products which are also economical.

2). **Let the market know about our product: Advertise**. We might have one of the best mail order products in the world, but if we don't make the market aware of it, our competition will run over us like a steamroller. We must advertise our product, and do so both effectively and consistently.

3). Running your business more efficiently. Such priorities might include streamlining our operation, cutting the fixed and variable costs, handling order shipping quickly and accurately, responding to customers' inquiry promptly, solving any billing and customer complaint issues effectively and immediately.

4). Having knowledge of the competition we face is a great help in rising above it. Such knowledge includes knowing where our company can effectively compete and where it should not compete. We can compete with retail stores by offering new and low priced gift items with good quality and reliable customer service.

5). Small firms that diversify often run the risk of losing the focus that created their success. One well-established product can of course be an important foundation in the early stages of our business. But according to past experience of mail order businesses such as a video game company owned by Gregory Fischbach, being a one-product company, no matter what the category is, places the company in a vulnerable position. Our philosophy is while are starting stage, stick with what we know best. We may have a variety of products but they are all going to be in the same category.

6). Find out whether our products are right for the growing elderly market, our competitors may be ignoring this group. More and more products are being designed these days to fit the special needs of the elderly market. Many of these products and services are right for older customers, while also remaining popular with younger buyers. Such products include watches with large numbers, easy-to-load cameras, and a device that uses an electric motor to raise a mattress and box spring off the bed frame.

7). Adapt ourselves and our business to meet the changing times. Giving our business and edge over our competition may well call for adjustment and adaptation. People in business can best face today's challenges, problems, and demands by learning how to change with the times.

8). Realize that today's customers and prospects expect and demand more value for their money. The decade of the 1990s will be remembered as the era when buyers and customers sought more value for their money. Buyers in general have become more sophisticated. Being aware of this fact, and acting on it as we operate our business can keep us ahead of our competition.

9). Consider making changes in existing products. We will be very sensitive about the new trends in our market and deliver the new ideas about the products to our suppliers and try to make changes to the products according to the preference of the customers.

10). Try to carve a new market and increase sales by capitalizing on changing demographics. We need to find out what are the trends in families, in schools, in workplaces, in people's social life. Keeping up with these trends can guide us to the right actions in our business.

Regulatory Restrictions

It is a federal offense to misrepresent your mail order company in any way. The postal delivery system is a branch of the federal government, and if you commit a felony through the mail, the U.S. Postal Service performs of its more unknown functions - that of a law enforcement authority.

The mail order restrictions and laws are mostly involving the following aspects:

1). Mail Order Advertising Law

2). Mail Order Sale Laws

3). Mail Order Fulfillment Laws

4). Mailing list Abuse.

You may contact the Direct Marketing Association or other mail order associations for a complete list of regulators in your area.

Chapter II:

Company and Products Description

Nature of Business

Fortune Star International Inc. will be a San Diego-based mail order corporation and owned by Gordon to sell unique gift products through online shopping channels and other catalog marketing procedures to the continent of United States.

Legal Form of the Business

Fortune Star will be formed as a corporation since there are several advantages of forming a corporation:

- Barring any fraudulent acts on your part, your personal holdings are not placed in jeopardy. You can't be held personally liable for the corporation's debts.

- This is the only permanent legal form of business. A corporation exists independently of its owners. Business continues, even though the shareholders come and go.

- The corporation enjoys a more favorable income tax rate than the individual or partner, when your new company really starts to earn money. [9]

Other features of the corporate form of ownership include the fact that banks and other lenders are far more attracted to the corporation than to sole proprietorships or partnerships. Of course, just like other business legal forms such as sole proprietorship and partnership, corporation has its drawbacks also. Yet considering the benefits of a corporation, it is more worth it to form a corporation.

To open a corporation, we will follow the legal requirements by the city of San Diego and by the State of California. First we need to get a business license form the City Treasurer, and then we need to get our fictitious business name registered. We need to put a statement in a local newspaper informing the public about the legal existence of our business. We then need to file a certificate of incorporation in the state of California which our business headquarters is located. We also need to acquire a California Seller's Permit from the State Board of Equalization since we sell taxable merchandise. We will also need to pay a fee to the state annually for incorporating, and another fee for conducting business in this form. We will consult with a business attorney for the detail procedures and proposals.

Company Objective

Our company's objective is to get our company's name recognized and accepted by customers thus increase our sales and expand our market share through effective advertising and marketing of our products.

Company Distinctive Competencies

Based on the fact that more and more people are shopping through mail order to meet all kinds of their personal needs for the convenience and the time saving as well as the competitive prices of the mail order system, Fortune Star International Inc. will be formed to satisfy the customers with unique and affordable gift items such decorative items, personal appliance items and collection items and etc. To achieve our goal, we will run our business with products of good quality and low prices, creative design, specialty items, satisfactory customer service, efficient management, and effective marketing methods. Our most distinctive competencies which will be the primary factors to contribute to our success are our strong back up from our products suppliers. Fortune Star International Inc. has signed contracts with over 10 manufacturers of gift and art products in China to be their North America distributors. We will get the factory prices from them to market their products and we also conduct the North America

Market research for them which enable us to give the manufacturers the latest market information of what is in demand and what is hot so they are able to adjust their prices and their designs and productions to meet the requirement of the market. We thus will have not only the newest products on the market, but also the best prices. In the highly competitive world of retail market, price places the vital part of winning the competition. In addition to the price, customer service will be our first priority to run the business. We will provide quick delivery, money back and exchange guarantee, prompt return to customers' questions and complaints. We also offer discount prices to large orders and sale prices during the holiday seasons to boost our sale.

Products Description

Rarely can a direct marketing firm succeed over the long term with only one product, no matter how popular the item may prove to be. You need to think in terms of a number of products. Most likely, you'll spend a considerable sum of money advertising your first item or two in the print media, in cyberspace or perhaps through direct mail. It would be a terrible waster of investment if you failed to follow up by seeking additional sales from those buyers. That is why we are going to promote one or two major products and expand our customer bank first, and then start launching more variety of products in the same category. The following is a brief introduction of the functions, benefits, ability to meet customer needs of several of our products.

1). Musical and Talking Clocks

These colorfully designed clocks are perfect for gift to children. They are designed into shapes of all kinds of animals and figures, they play several different tones of music and announce the time in English at each hour with the animal imitating voice. They can be set so that they will only make the sound during a certain period of time suppose 7: am to 8: pm. The material is plastic and they are light in weight so they are safe from dropping to the ground or playing around by smaller kids. Smaller children can learn a great deal about how to tell time and how to count numbers and it can greatly increase children's curiosity to learn new things and to use their imaginations. Please see product exhibit 1 in Appendix B for detail.

2). Fine Porcelain Figures

Those fun Bride and Groom figures are perfect for wedding gift or to couples in love. They are high quality hand craft porcelain figures with rich facial expressions and bright colors. They are detailed craft and some of them come with a matching lamp. They are easy to clean and have collection values.

3). Micro Towel

Adopted the advanced equipment and technology, the superior towel of pure cotton is compressed and refined with special technique as various new and peculiar micro-styles with circular, heart, five-pointed star, animal and geometry shapes after the processing of deep purification and sterilizing with infrared ray, the outstanding features are: small and exquisite, convenient and practical, healthy and clean. Micro towels are ideal as gifts or for personal use. They are suitable for hotels, restaurants, and companies to print their ads. And logo and as give away items to customers and potential prospects to promote their business. Please see product exhibit 3 in Appendix B.

4). Decoration Art pieces

These are all very creatively designed, delicate crafted items like swing horses with clocks, desk top globes, moving geometric artworks, and desk pen holders. They are amazingly beautiful and elegant and they are perfect for gift to bosses, secretaries, colleagues, as well as college students.

5). Name Chop Seals

Beautifully carved stones with animal symbols on the top to represent the twelve animals, representing the twelve Earthkt Branches, used to symbolize the year in which a person is born. Those stones can be ordered by the customers with their name carved in artistic Chinese characters at the bottom of the stones so that they can use them to stamp on their art works, their books, their post cards and their possession to give them the individualism and collection value. These stone seals have not only the practical use but also the collection value. More and more American people are getting to know about this unique ancient Chinese art. Lucily, we are the only few people in America who are the expert artists to possess the special skills of engraving the stone stamps into artistic ancient Chinese characters. They are highly specialized products and we have the great advantages in successfully marketing them. They have been proved to be profit making products for us in the past.

To summarize the characteristics of our mail order products, they can be described as follows:

- They are unique, unusual, interesting.

- They are not readily available in stores.

- They offer good value for the price.

- They provide - as the very minimum - a gross margin percentage of between 40 to 60 percent of the selling price.

- They are easy to mail or ship.

- The mailing /shipping cost is modest.

- A potential for repeat orders exist.

Product Life Cycle

Every product has its life cycle which has four cycle stages. First, it is in the introductory stage which means it is a newly born product and needs time to be promoted and recognized; then, it will enter into the growth stage which is the most promising time of the product. It is in high demand and the price is usually high. After a certain period of growth, the product will reach its maturity stage which is the prime time of the product's life. It has been well recognized by the market at this time. The product wills eventually going into the decline stage which means the demand is down and it has been replaced by something new again. After extensive examination and research on market demand, sales, costs, and profits they generate, we conclude that our products are in the introduction and growth stage of a product life cycle which is the best time to get into. Yet, we need to spend major time and capital to develop the market for them.

Chapter III:

Marketing and Sales Activities

Overall Marketing Strategy

Fortune Star International's overall marketing strategy is to use the efficient and effective medium to introduce its products to the customers and to generate the sales targets projected on a monthly and yearly basis. However, our major marketing strategy will be focused on marketing through the Internet because of its effectiveness and low cost and the huge amount of readers it can reach. Actually, we think marketing on-line is the best marketing vehicle for mail order business starters. We will discuss Internet marketing plan in more detail later on. First, we will discuss some of the marketing guidelines we follow.

1). Explore free and low cost marketing opportunities:

As the beginner in a new business, it is not wise and financially permitted to spend a lot of money to advertise in every possible medium you can find in the market. Too many people jump into a mail order business with an expensive, flashy full-page ad in a big magazine which costs thousands of dollars. It is great if it is successful, but what do you do when your ad only pulls enough orders to cover its cost, and you have no marketing budget left for new ads? The smart thing to do at the start is to take advantage of all the free and low cost marketing options at your fingertips. Fortune Star International will take full advantage of the free and low cost marketing opportunities such as advertising on the Internet, free press release, newsletters, brochures, circulars, business cards. We truly believe that "Advertising doesn't have to be expensive to be effective."[10]

2). Do small scale tests before large scale advertising

Before we spend large amount of money into a large ad or mailing, we will place smaller ad with the same message in the magazine or journal for two or three issues, and see if it pulls. If it works, it is great and we may put a lot larger ad next time. If it doesn't work, it will permit us to figure out why it did not work. Either the ad isn't effective or we are reaching the wrong audience. Review it and find out the new direction. [11]

3). Tracking the ads

Keying and tracking ads is simple and important. It tells you which ad you run generate the most response and orders. If it is so effectively, of course we want to concentrate more on this type of ad in the future. What we will do is on each ad, we will add a letter or number code following our return address that will indicate to us where the order came from. We will also make a chart in the computer with columns for date, item ordered, amount paid, and date the order was shipped. At the top of the page, we will write down the ad code next to it. Then, when we receive orders, record the information on the proper page. [12]

Communication

1). Promotion: In order to attract potential buyers' interest in buying our products, we have special sale prices offered at holiday seasons and special occasions as well as a weekly special product promotion through our online company website, our cybermall site, and our advertisement in the newspapers and magazines. We will also offer free gift items if customers order over a certain amount of dollars. The free gifts will be attractive and practical items which add the motivation for people to buy. In order to transfer a buyer into a long term customer, we will offer special discount to anyone who buys more than one time. If the buyer liked what he or she bought from us, there is a good chance that we can sell more than once to a customer.

Anyway, we will make our buyers feel good about doing business with us and they will make themselves regular customers.

2). Public Relations: We will participate in related product trade shows and fairs to exhibit our products and expose ourselves to the public. It is also a very effective way to locate individual and wholesale distributors who frequently go to the trade shows to find new products and new suppliers. We will communicate with customers or people who are interested in knowing more about our products through e-mail. We encourage them to write to us to give their opinions about our products.

3). Printed materials: In addition to the ad. In the newspapers and magazine, we will print a certain amount of product catalogues and mail order brochures for distribution and direct mail to companies, hotels, distributors, retail shops and individuals who are the prospective customers. We will provide our telephone number, our fax number, our e-mail address, and our P.O. Box mailing address in those materials so the customers can call, fax or mail the response cards to make their orders.

Marketing on the Internet

Cambridge, Mass. based Forester Research, Inc. completed a survey of Internet merchants in April, 1996. "On-line retailing is finally gaining traction," according to the survey, Internet sales were estimated at $51.8 million for that year. Also, according to the study, entrepreneurs are achieving the most success by marketing on-line. By the year 2000, sales should reach $6.6 billion. According to another recent report by Bizsource Technology Association, [13] approximately 113 million people around the world have access to the Internet now. Some 62 million Americans, 20 million Europeans and 14 million Asians/Middle Easterners are now online. From the information above, we clearly realize that advertising through the Internet is going to be the most cost effective place to market our mail order products. The number of people we can reach with our advertisement is over 62 million people now.

Therefore, marketing on the Internet offers many advantages for companies that want to sell products. Here are several reasons for a mail order business to advertise its products/services on line:

- Reach a worldwide audience. People worldwide can read the information on your site and decide to start a business relationship with you.

- Do business with an affluent market. Reports show that the first wave of Internet citizens makes more money and have completed higher education levels than the average American.

- No barrier of time zones, people can read it 24 hours a day, 7 days a week.

- Deal with consumers when they are ready to buy. Customers come to your site when they begin the buying process. Either they are comparing your product to competitors or they have the desire to buy directly from you.

- Enjoy low cost of advertising. The World Wide Web is the least expensive printing press ever invented. Merchants have an unlimited amount of space to describe and demonstrate their entire range of products.

- Create specialized sales scripts appealing to each type of consumer, using their unique buying buzz words. With the advantages of hyperlinking information, pictures, sound, and video, merchants can create customized sales presentations.

- Interact with customers and generate inquiries. People read your ad on your Web site can let you know they are interested in learning more.[14]

- Create lists of qualified prospects. Prospects who visit your home page or request information via e-mail can be added to your e-mail lists and databases.

- Make sales directly over the Internet, or by phone, mail or fax.

- Sell to targeted audiences with lifestyle interest. [15]

Developing Effective Channels for Online Sales

Selling online is defined as an actual sales transaction taking place - a buyer filling out some sort of an online order form and agreeing to price and payment terms. Online advertising and online sales are closely bounded. One parallel is mail order advertising in which a consumer responds to advertising and then may place an order using a reply form or coupon. In the same way, online advertising can act as a kind of doorway leading to an electronic order form where a purchase takes place. It is no secret that a growing number of mail order entrepreneurs are looking for the right way to use new media to sell their products and services. The primary consideration is finding a sales format that fits your product and your company's approach to the marketplace.[16] Fortune Star International will test the following on line marketing formats to promote our business.

1). Renting space in the Internet Shopping Mall: Many online users enjoy shopping directly from their computers, and they've been doing so for years. According to Modem Media, a Connecticut-based advertising and research agency, the top ten of the 150 merchants selling on consumer-oriented online services in 1993 generated 80 percent of the $50 million in sales made by vendors on the major online shopping malls. Larger merchants generate an average of $3 million annually from online sales, while medium-size merchants earn about $500,000 and small merchants around $83,000.

The online shopping malls like choice mall arrange the companies into departments and floors, based on what they sell. [17] To be included on the list, we need to send a message describing what we are selling and our company's Internet address. For detailed list of shopping malls, please see appendix C. The list is also available on the Web at *http://www.mecklerweb.com*.

As an online merchant, we have to keep our site information up-to-date and we have to give online users reasons to visit and then return to our store - for example, promotion, advertising, special sales, etc.

2). ***Selling on the Internet through a broker***: On line sales brokers like eBay is an Internet-based product purchasing broker. It is also another online service we are going to test our sales. We'll sign up with them as a seller with a small monthly fee. Once we opened the account with them, they will list our product and pictures into their shopping site classified by what we sell. When the buyers enter into their site and decide to buy our products, they will fill a purchase form with their payment information to eBay. When eBay receive their payment, they will e-mail the order to us and we send the products to the buyers. eBay will charge us a small percentage of broker fee for each item we sell. In this way, we do not need to worry about fraud checks since the online broker has already taken care it for us. We just ship our products to the customers and get the payment from the broker. For more information, you may reach their website at *http://www.ebay.com*.

3). ***Creating our own website***: In order to promote our mail order business successfully and establish our own reputation in the mail order world, we need to create our own website. We will work together with a web design consultant since they have designed websites for other companies before and they will be able to draw on that experience to create a better presentation for us. By using HTML which web documents are formatted, we will be able to introduce information about our company, our products in a more detailed and professional image. The customers will be able to interact with us directly. In the home page which is the first page visitors will see when they access our site, we will include brief descriptions of each option for additional information that can be accessed from that page. We will include the following information into our website.

- Name of our company

- Logo

- Mission Statement - explains what our business does and the market it serves.

- Sales - Tells people at a glance what the hot buys are this week.

- What's new - tells viewers what information has been added or changed.

- Message from the president - can show true character and nature of the company, giving it a personal feel.

- Catalogs - show the full range of products in our store, with descriptions, prices, and ordering information as well as transaction capabilities.

- Order form- asks the buyers to provide their information such as name, address, phone number, products they order, and payment information.

- E-mail response form - so people can contact us directly and create a one-on-one customer relationship.

- Contact Information- our company's mail box address, telephone, and fax number. This information should be included in all pages since people print out individual pages, not the entire site.

Online Sales Activities

1). When a buyer responds to our company website, he will send in a check or call and verbally transmits a credit card number over the telephone. This is fairly the traditional approach, and no financial transaction takes place on the net. The consumer can also print out our online order form and leave his or her credit card number and sign the form. With this approach, the consumer feels more secure with his credit card information and it is also good for us since they signed the form. We will encourage them to use the latter.

2). When the consumer sets up an account with our online shopping mall manager or our online broker, he or she leaves his or her credit card number by means other than the net, and gives the third party the authorization to bill the account whenever the consumer chooses to buy something.

Chapter IV:

Operation

In general, we will provide the basic customer service conveniences which are toll-free number, credit card acceptance, overnight and two-day shipping options, satisfaction guaranteed statements, 24-hour-a-day, 7-day-a-week service, and environmentally friendly packaging and catalogs. Follow these tried-and-true methods for achieving customer service satisfaction, and we are sure that we will see results in the volume of sales we make.

Product Delivery Procedures

1. Before the delivery

After we receive customer's order either through the mail, fax, toll-free phone call or online e-mail, we will process the order by the type of product he or she ordered the same day. We will make sure we deposit the checks to our bank and process credit-card charges the same day. The most important issue mail order businesses should pay attention is to make sure to get paid before the shipping of the products. We will take the following steps before the delivery in order to avoid financial losses.

- **Wait for each deposited item to "clear"** - be paid by the bank or other entity on which it is drawn and be sure to explain to each customer that we will clear the check first before shipping. They will understand because they've been victims of bounced checks themselves.

- **Process each credit-card charge before we ship** - sometimes people charge over their card limit and additional charges will not go through. We have to make sure that the payment is made by the cardholder to the bank. Our bank can help us to set up the credit line to accept credit cards and loan us a terminal to process the cards.

- **Ship only when money order clears** - don't automatically assume that money orders never bounce. Sometime, money orders will turn out to be counterfeited ones. So we have to take caution to protect our business.

2). Packaging

We will use the standard mail packaging boxes required by our delivery carriers. The packaging material must be safe and durable.

3). Delivery Carriers

Immediately after we cleared the checks and charged the card, we will make sure we will deliver the products they ordered the same day or next morning if it already passed the delivery time the same day. When people order something from the mail, they want to have it right away. So in order to win in the mail order business, we have to have a quick delivery service. Today, we have a number of options for the best mail order delivery of any item ordered from us. We will use UPS to do most of our delivery. The advantages with UPS delivery are:

- We can have our packages picked up every day at a small extra cost to us.
- Some UPS rates are lower than the post office rates to the same address.
- Insurance is automatically included (up to $100) on all UPS shipments.
- UPS will accept our company check in payment for the shipping. This is not always so at the post office.
- UPS will deliver COD (Cash on Delivery) orders and accept a check in payment.
- For local delivery UPS seems to be faster than other type of delivery.

We will get evidence of delivery for every item we shipped. We will always get a signed receipt showing the item was received by the addressee.

4). Keeping Record

When an order arrived by mail, it must be processed. Each envelope is date-stamped with the arrival date. Then the item ordered is marked on the outside of the envelope, along with the amount enclosed, and the type of payment - a check, money order or charge by credit card. Then envelopes containing regular checks and money orders are set aside to allow time for each check to clear. Local checks require less clearance time than checks drawn on distant banks. So local checks get quicker shipment. Once the check clears, the order is entered into our customer record in the computer, a ship label is printed out and applied to the package containing the item ordered. The package is then shipped via UPS. Credit card charges will first be processed by dialing the number to verify the information and make sure that charge will go through. Once that is done, the shipment process will be the same as above.

Telephone orders are handled a little bit different. The customer calls in and orders one or more items, paying by credit card. Information on the customer (name, address, telephone number, credit card number, and expiration date) is obtained by the person answering the phone. Next, the card number, expiration date, and amount of the charge are keyed into the Electronic Data Capture terminal. Instant approval, or disapproval, is obtained, along with the authorization number for approved transactions. A charge ticket is prepared for mailing to the customer. Then the order is entered in computer, as above, and the order is shipped.

Operating Competitive Advantages

Our most operating competitive advantage is our low direct costs. Since Fortune Star International will be a home-based mail order business, we do not need to spend thousands of dollars to rent a space to start our business. We can use part of our 3-car garage as well as another room as storage place. We will only have moderate amount of inventory to start with. Once we open the market, we will have a relatively larger inventory. When that happens, we will rent a self-storage space to keep our inventory. The storage fee will be much less than a warehouse. We will utilize the "Just in Time" inventory method to control our inventory. It is the best way to prevent high inventory cost and a financial loss. In addition, we do not need to hire many people to operate the business.

Suppliers

As mentioned earlier, our product suppliers are one of our most competitive advantages. They are manufacturers located in different region of China. We already have established strong relationships with more than a dozen of them because of our long term connections with them. We have distribution and market development agreements with them to promote their products in the United States. We also provide overseas market investigation for them. Based on all the above relations, we are able to get factory prices and new market development incentives from them. Even though, at the beginning we won't order large amount of products since we are developing the market and test the water, we still can enjoy the special incentives from them as agreed in the contracts. These manufacturers are all financially strong and have the ability to fill large or small order on time. So they are reliable suppliers to us as long as we give them enough time to get the shipment ready. The lead time they require is usually around 30 to 45 days since they have to ship our order by ocean cargo. One of our concerns is that in case we need some supply in a hurry, we won't have enough time to get them shipped to us right away. Another concern we have is the fact that our suppliers' goal is to get large orders from distributors like us in order to make their profit. So in order to keep our competitive prices for the long term, we need to expand our business and be able to increase our order quantity from our suppliers in the future. That's why we have the vision in our mind that we are going to expand our business into professional drop shipper who supply merchandise to other mail order dealers. We will buy merchandise in wholesale quantities and maintain a constant stock of merchandise and fill orders for small dealers since majority of mail order business in the United States are performed by people on a part time basis and few buy their merchandise in large wholesale quantities. We realize that a stable and long term relationship with our suppliers is very critical to the success of our business. We will take any effort to enhance our relationship with them. Once our business developed into certain size, we will consider being shareholder partners with some of our suppliers and acquisition of some key suppliers.

Chapter V:

Management and Ownership

Management Mission

Through effective and efficient management effort to gain market recognition, reduce operation cost, increase net income, offer satisfactory customer service, and to gain customer loyalty and increase sales of Fortune Star International, Inc.

Management Staff Structure

Fortune Star Inc. will be owned by Mr. Gordon and co-owned by Ms. Helen. There are two managers in the company. Ms. Helen is Manager of Sales & Marketing and Mr. Biao will be Manager of Purchasing. The following are the brief introduction of each staff member and their responsibilities.

Owner

Mr. Gordon will be the President of Fortune Star International, Inc. He is in charge of the business planning and overall administration and operation of the company. He controls capital spending and forecast sales growth. He oversees all the financial information such as monthly balance statement, cash flow analysis and income statement. He is responsible for hiring management level staff. He is the founder of the company and contributes his own capital to start the business. Mr. Gordon got his MBA degree from National University in San Diego, California. He offers over 10 years of experience in business operation and business management. He has strong work ethics and once he undertakes a job, no matter big or small, he is determined to do a very good job. He is energetic, athletic, hardworking, and always full of hope for the future.

Key Managers

Helen will be the General Manager and the co-owner of Fortune Star International, Inc. She will be responsible for sales & marketing and customer relations. Her primary duties will be writing advertising messages and product descriptions for catalogs, brochures, publications, magazines, and newsletters; Locating the right medium to advertise and market our products; Communicating and coordinating with advertising medium. She offers 10 years track record of marketing, networking, sales, international marketing and sales of consumer products and light industrial products in the domestic and international marketplace. She successfully promoted, established, coordinated and facilitating various product distribution channels. She has been working for two years now as a marketing coordinator for a local marketing company. She is experienced in networking with distributors; organizing trade show participation; writing promotion and presentation materials; and coordinating and negotiating business deals. She also has over two year experience as a sales professional. Helen also worked as an overseas representative for a major industrial development corporation located in Canton China. Helen got her master's degree in International Relations from California State University. Helen has strong communication skills and experienced in dealing with customer issues. She has sharp ideas about what will sell and how to sell it. She is going to be the main contributor to our business.

Mr. Biao is our Overseas Purchasing Manager and he is responsible for all the major activities with the supply of our merchandise. His main duties include communicating and negotiating prices with the suppliers, taking care order fulfillment, controlling product quality, arranging shipping of products. Mr. Biao has been working for over ten years as a loan officer in Chinese Construction Bank, Shenzhen Branch. He has rich connections and resources with Chinese manufacturers, wholesalers, and import and export companies. He is very experienced in locating product resources and negotiating the most competitive prices to fill wholesale and import orders. He can locate the most reliable freight forwarders and get good deals with shipping. He also has great knowledge in dealing with financial issues. He will play an important role in supplying our company good quality products with competitive prices.

Chapter VI:

Financial Analysis

Start-Up Cost

The start - up cost of Fortune Star International Inc. consists of the following:

1). Business Registration and License Fee: All the fee involved in registering the business.

2). Corporation Filing Consulting Fee: Include consulting fee to the business lawyer to draft our corporation filing form.

3). Initial Inventory: We will buy a test amount of inventory of the five types of products we are going to launch. The cost will include inventory purchase and shipping and import tariff and broker fee.

4). Catalogs, Newsletter, Brochures: Include cost of the all the initial printing and copying of product introductory catalogs, mail order newsletter and brochures.

5). Media Advertising: Include advertising in magazines and direct mail catalogs, renting shopping mall space on the Internet, designing company website.

6). Operation Supplies: Include a credit card terminal, a picture scanner, stationary.

7). Mail Delivery Supplies: Include wrapping material and mail boxes, address stickers.

8). Opening Business Account: Include the monthly service fee and credit card transaction fee.

9). Miscellaneous Cost

Table 1

Start-Up Cost			
License Fee			$350
Corporation Filing Fee			$300
Initial Inventory			$3,800
Catalogs, Newsletter, Brochures			$600
Media Advertising			$1,900
Operation Supplies			$1,000
Mail Delivery Supplies			$300
Opening Business Account			$100
Basic Salaries			$3,000
Miscellaneous Cost			$1,000
Subtotal Total			$12,350

Funds Required and Their Uses

It is true that in order to make money, you have to have money. Any business must run on money, even launching a modest, part-time, home-based venture requires some financial support. This is just as true with a mail order business as it is with any other type of enterprise. Luckily, mail order business doesn't call for a heavy initial investment as most other businesses do.

Based on the Start-Up cost statement, total funds needed to start our mail order business are around $12,350.00. The owner will invest his own saving of $5350.00 and the rest $7000.00 will be financed through a home equity loan with an interest rate of 7.5% which is expected to be paid off in a year. The monthly interest payment will be $43.75. ($7000 x 7.5% / 12)

Product Pricing

Price setting for our products is very critical to the success of our mail order business. In order to survive the competition and win the customers, a reasonable price plays a very important role. Every item we carry should be priced to cover its cost, freight charges, an appropriate share of our overhead (fixed and variable operating expenses), and a reasonable profit. In reality, some items will warrant a high gross profit, and others require a low profit in order to move them quickly. As long as the aggregate gross and net profits are sufficiently high, our business should be successful.

In order to set a reasonable price, we have taken into consideration of the following factors in pricing:

- Level of customer demand.

- Value, as perceived by buyers.

- Competitors' prices.

- State of the economy.

- Newness of the product or service.

In addition to the above factors, we must devote close attention to other aspects that are crucial to this type of business: gross margin and promotional costs. We need to set selling prices on our offerings that will bring in enough total gross margin dollars to cover our cost of goods, all advertising expenditures, and all operating costs-and still leave us with a reasonable amount of profit.

Based on the above information, we come up with the following prices for our products with a minimum of 100 % mark up to cover the cost of goods, fix and variable expenses and to leave us a fair amount of profit.

Table 2

Merchandise Prices							
Product Name							Unit Price
Musical & Talking Clock							$19.50
Fine Porcelain Figure							$9.95
Micro Towel							$2.95
Swinging Horse							$25.95
Pen Holder							$29.95
Name Chop							$45

Sales Forecast

We predict our mail order sales for the first six month will be moderate and we expect to make only a fair profit but not a fortune for the first year. It is based on the fact that for the first 6 months, most of the small businesses are trying to get their products known and recognized by the customers and they have not established their market share yet. The following is our sales forecast on a monthly for the first one year starting from January 1, 1999.

Table 3

Sales Forecast							
		January	February	March	April	May	June
Musical & Talking Clock							
Units Sold		180	210	255	270	280	285
Price Per Unit		$19.95	$19.95	$19.95	$19.95	$19.95	$19.95
Total Sales		$3,591	$4,189.50	$5,087.25	$5,386.50	$5,586	$5,685.75
Fine Porcelain Figure							
Units Sold		150	160	165	170	180	180
Price Per Unit		$9.95	$9.95	$9.95	$9.95	$9.95	$9.95
Total Sales		$1,492.50	$1,592	$1,641.75	$1,691.50	$1,791	$1,791
Total Sales (Two Products)		$5,084	$5,781.50	$6,729.00	$7,078.00	$7,377.00	$7,476.75

Sales Forecast							
		July	August	September	October	November	December
Musical & Talking Clock							
Units Sold		270	285	350	400	450	500
Price Per Unit		$19.95	$19.95	$19.95	$19.95	$19.95	$19.95
Total Sales		$5,386.50	$5,386.50	$5,386.50	$5,386.50	$5,386.50	$5,386.50
Fine Porcelain Figure							
Units Sold		180	190	200	285	310	315
Price Per Unit		$9.95	$9.95	$9.95	$9.95	$9.95	$9.95
Total Sales (Two Products)		$1,791	$1,891	$1,940	$1,841	$2,090	$2,139
Total Sales (Two Products)		$7,177.50	$7,277.00	$7,326.75	$7,227.25	$7,476.00	$7,525.75

Table 4

Cost Of Good Sold						
	January	February	March	April	May	June
Musical & Talking Clock						
Units Sold	180	210	255	270	280	285
Price Per Unit	$7.50	$7.50	$7.50	$7.50	$7.50	$7.50
Total Sales	$1,350	$1,575	$1,913	$2,025	$2,100	$2,138
Fine Porcelain Figure						
Units Sold	150	160	165	170	180	180
Price Per Unit	$3.30	$3.30	$3.30	$3.30	$3.30	$3.30
Total Sales	$495.00	$528.00	$544.50	$561.00	$594.00	$594.00
Total Sales (Two Products)	$1,845	$2,103	$2,457	$2,586	$2,694	$2,732

Cost Of Good Sold						
	July	August	September	October	November	December
Musical & Talking Clock						
Units Sold	270	285	280	270	285	315
Price Per Unit	$7.50	$7.50	$7.50	$7.50	$7.50	$7.50
Total Sales	$2,025.00	$2,137.50	$2,100.00	$2,025.00	$2,137.50	$2,362.50
Fine Porcelain Figure						
Units Sold	180	190	195	185	210	215
Price Per Unit	$3.30	$3.30	$3.30	$3.30	$3.30	$3.30
Total Sales (Two Products)	$594	$627	$644	$611	$693	$710
Total Sales (Two Products)	$2,619.00	$2,764.50	$2,743.50	$2,635.50	$2,830.50	$3,072.00

Table 5

Income Statement: Annual By Month							
For Year: 1999		**January**	**February**	**March**	**April**	**May**	**June**
Sales Revenues		$5,084.00	$5,781.50	$6,729.00	$7,078.00	$7,377.00	$7,476.75
Cost Of Good Sold		$1,845	$2,103	$2,457	$2,586	$2,694	$2,732
Gross Profit		$3,239.00	$3,678.50	$4,272.00	$4,492.00	$4,683.00	$4,744.75
General & Administration Expenses							
Salaries & Benefits & Payroll Taxes		$1,307	$1,307	$1,307	$1,307	$1,307	$1,307
Depreciation		$42	$42	$42	$42	$42	$42
Insurance		$41	$41	$41	$41	$41	$41
Electricity		$38	$38	$38	$38	$38	$38
Telephone		$125	$125	$125	$125	$125	$125
Office Supplies		$83	$83	$83	$83	$83	$83
Marketing And Advertising		$158	$158	$158	$158	$158	$158
Total G & A Expenses		$1,794	$1,794	$1,794	$1,794	$1,794	$1,794
Net Income Before Taxes		$1,445	$1,885	$2,478	$2,698	$2,889	$2,951
Taxes		$216.75	$282.68	$371.70	$404.70	$433.35	$442.61
Net Income After Taxes		$1,228.25	$1,601.83	$2,106.30	$2,293.30	$2,455.65	$2,508.14

For Year: 1999		**July**	**August**	**September**	**October**	**November**	**December**
Sales Revenues		$7,177.50	$7,277.00	$7,326.75	$7,227.25	$7,476.00	$7,525.75
Cost Of Good Sold		$2,619.00	$2,764.50	$2,743.50	$2,635.50	$2,830.50	$3,072.00
Gross Profit		$4,558.50	$4,512.50	$4,583.25	$4,591.75	$4,645.50	$4,453.75
General & administration Expenses							
Salaries & Benefits & Payroll Taxes		$1,307	$1,307	$1,307	$1,307	$1,307	$1,307
Depreciation		$42	$42	$42	$42	$42	$42
Insurance		$41	$41	$41	$41	$41	$41
Electricity		$38	$38	$38	$38	$38	$38
Telephone		$125	$125	$125	$125	$125	$125
Office Supplies		$83	$83	$83	$83	$83	$83
Marketing And Advertising		$158	$158	$158	$158	$158	$158
Total G & A Expenses		$1,794	$1,794	$1,794	$1,794	$1,794	$1,794
Net Income Before Taxes		$2,764.50	$2,718.50	$2,789.25	$2,797.75	$2,851.50	$2,659.75
Taxes		$414.68	$407.78	$418.39	$419.66	$427.73	$398.96
Net Income After Taxes		$2,349.83	$2,310.73	$2,370.86	$2,378.09	$2,423.78	$2,260.79

Table 6

Income Statement: Annual Four Years	Yr. 1999	Yr. 2000	Yr. 2001	Yr. 2002
Sales Revenues	$83,536.50	$95,562.52	$110,893.12	$126,853.16
Cost Of Good Sold	$31,082	$35,587	$43,563	$50,865
Gross Profit	$52,454.50	$59,975.52	$67,330.12	$75,988.16
General And Administration Expenses				
Salaries & Benefits & Payroll Taxes	$15,681	$17,265	$20,253	$23,157
Depreciation	$500	$600	$700	$800
Insurance	$500	$500	$500	$500
Electricity	$450	$450	$450	$450
Telephone	$1,500	$1,780	$1,900	$2,000
Office Supplies	$1,000	$1,000	$1,000	$1,000
Marketing And Advertising	$1,900	$2,500	$2,800	$3,000
Total G & A Expenses	$21,531	$24,095	$27,603	$30,907
Net Income Before Taxes	$30,923.50	$35,880.52	$39,727.12	$45,081.16
Taxes	$4,638.53	$5,382.08	$5,959.07	$6,762.17
Net Income After Taxes	$26,284.98	$30,498.44	$33,768.05	$38,318.99

Break Even Analysis for 1999

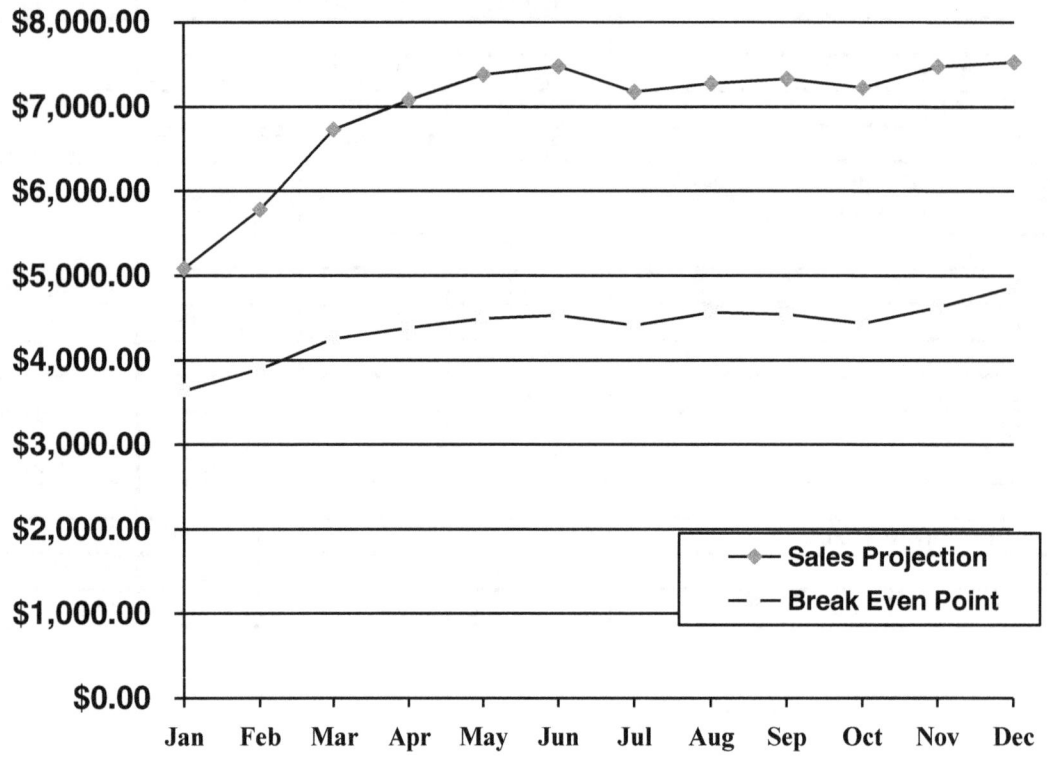

Chapter VII: Conclusion

Through effort and persistence, we are confident that we will manage to establish and build a strong, exciting new business. It may take us three to five years to accomplish it, overcoming countless difficulties, but we will get there. Our goal is to do develop into a multi-million wholesale and distribution center in ten year. The mail order business is the first step to make it happen. In order to operate a successful business, it is very important to spend time to study and research the industry, the market, the customer, the product, the sales and marketing strategy, how the business is going to be operated, and all the financial evaluations before we get into the business.   Based on those data and information we collected, we then need to draft a business plan with clear goals to direct us in our new business endeavor. Without a business plan, a business is going to be like a car without a driver. It will hit around and get to nowhere. A business plan gives us a vision of the whole picture and it can point out what strengths and weaknesses we have in operating our new business and where our business is going five years, ten years from now. The business plan here covers all the major issues we are going to face in building our mail order business, yet it is only a preliminary outline, it will be enriched and upgraded gradually with the start-up and the build-up of our business. It is not only going to serve as a valuable management tool to evaluate and control our company's performance but also as our company's message to our suppliers, lenders and potential investors into our business.

REFERENCES

Book:

Alfred, G. (1995). The Little Online Book. Berkeley, CA: Peachpit Press.

Alfred & Emily, G. (1995). Making Money on the Internet. New York, NY: McGraw- Hill, Inc.

Bernadette, T. (1996). Start Smart Your Home-Based Business. New York, NY: A Macmillan Spectrum Book.

Cecil, C.H. (1988). Mail Order Moonlighting. Berkeley, CA: Ten Speed Press.

David, A. & Brent, H. (1995). The Internet Business Companion. Reading, MA: Addison-Wesley Publishing Co.

Daniel, S. (1997). Online Marketing Handbook. New York, NY: Van Nostrand Reinhold.

Daniel, S. (1996). 101 Businesses You Can Start on the Internet. New York, NY: Van Nostrand Reinhold.

Douglas, E. (1997). The Internet Book. Upper Saddle River, NJ: Prentice-Hall, Inc.

Eugene, M. (1997). Web Visions. New York, NY: Van Nostrand Reinhold.

Greg, H. (1997). Increasing Hits and Selling More on Your Web Site. New York, NY: Wiley Computer Publishing.

Irving, B. (1995). Mail Order Selling. New York, NY: John Wiley & Sons, Inc.

Jay Conrad, L. & Charles, R. (1996). Guerrilla Marketing Online Weapons. New York, New York: Houghton Mifflin.

Janice, M.K. & Paul, K. James, H.M. (1997). Web Marketing Cook Book. New York, NY: Wiley Computer Publishing.

Julian, S. (1993). How to Start and Operate A Mail-Order Business. New York, NY: McGraw-Hill, Inc.

Len, K. (1995). Cyber Marketing. New York, NY: Amacom.

L. Perry Wilbur. (1993). Money in Your Mailbox. New York, NY: John Wiley & Sons, Inc.

Martha, S. (1997). How to Make a Fortune on the Internet. New York, New York: Harper Perennial Inc.

Paul, J., Thomas, J.K. and Joshua, O.T. (1996). Web Advertising and Marketing. Rocklin, CA. Prima Publishing.

Tyler, G (1987). <u>How to Start Your Own Business on A Shoestring and Make up to $500,000 a Year</u>. Rocklin, CA: Prima Publishing & Communications.

Tyler, G. (1992). <u>Mail Order Success Secrets</u>. New York, NY: Prima Publishing.

Tyler, G. (1996). <u>101 Great Mail-Order Businesses</u>. Rocklin, CA: Prima Publishing.

Vince, E. (1995). How<u> to Grow Your Business on the Internet</u>. Scottsdale, AZ: Coriolis Group Books.

Wilbur, M. Y. (1996). <u>A Basic Guide for Valuing a Company</u>. New York, N.Y: John Wiley & Sons, Inc.

William, A. (1996). <u>Building A Mail Order Business</u>. New York, NY: John Wiley & Sons, Inc.

Winn, S. & Chris, G. (1996). <u>Complete Internet Business Toolkit</u>. New York, NY: Van Nostrand Reinhold.

Article:

Pamela, R. (May, 1998) Start a business with $5,000 or less? <u>Income Opportunities</u>. v.63 n.5 p19-28.

Karen, L.M. (Nov, 1997) Post It For Free. <u>Small Business Computing. v.15 n.11 p49-52</u>

Internet:

Internet Mail-Order News - What is Mail Order? Dale, R.

<u>http://www.</u> homeincome.com/homebased/internet-mon/page5.htm

Photographic Mail Order Survey

<u>http://www.</u> compsolv.com/los/pmos.shtml

On-Line Order Form

<u>http://gamblersbook.com/neweorder.htm</u>

How You Can Become a Mail-Order Drop-Shipper

<u>http://www.homeincome.com/homebiz/magazines/drop-shippers.htm</u>

The following is a list of some high-profile, well-designed Web cybermalls.

Exhibit 3.1 Cybermalls with Space to Rent

- *Branch Mall* at *<u>http://branch.com</u>*. The Branch Mall is one of the original Web cybermalls, with a long list of active merchants at its site. 313-741-4442.

- *CommerceNet* at *http://www.commerce.net*. CommerceNet is supported by a nonprofit consortium of major high-tech companies committed to the concept of electronic commerce. 415-617-8790.

- CTS Net at *http://www.cts.com*. CTS Net is the Web mall of a San Diego-based Internet service provider. 619-637-3637 or *webmaster@cts.com*

- *Downtown Anywhere* at *http://www.awa.com*. This is a friendly-looking, well-organized, community-like commercial site. 617-522-8102 or downtown@awa.com

- *First Virtual Holdings, Inc.,* at *http://www.fv.com*. First Virtual's site demonstrates the company's unique approach to electronic commerce. 307-638-3688

- *Global Network Navigator* at *http://gnn.com*. GNN is a high-traffic commercial site that also includes pointers to a wide variety of resources on the Internet. 707-829-0515.

- *Internet Distribution Services* at *http://www.service.com*. The operators of this site have helped to design some of the most attractive and effective commercial sites on the Web. 415-856-8265.

- Internet Shopping Network at http://www.internet.net. Cable TV's Home Shopping Network owns this web network. They have a wide product line. 415-617-0595

- *Online Computer Marketplace* at *http://www.ocm.com*. This site features merchants who sell computer products and computer services. 508-48-0577.

- *Open Market, Inc.* at *http://www.openmarket.com*. Their approach is to help companies easily set up a storefront in cyberspace, using their StoreBuilder system. 617-621-9500 or *info@openmarket.com*.

Shopping 2000 at http://www.shopping2000.com. Shopping 2000 features over forty major retailers and direct mail catalog merchants-be sure to visit this site. 212-447.9494.

HOW TO BUILD AND DEVELOP AMAIL ORDER BUSINESS

The Concept is going to be a home-based mail order business selling gift items mainly through Internet advertising and have the products delivered to the homes across the whole United States. The Concept is to offer refreshing and creative gift products not readily to find at the stores and have them delivered right to the homes of customers. It offers not only the convenience of shopping but also the opportunity to get unique gift ideas at a very reasonable price. Currently in the United States, more and more people are doing mail order business at their home. In fact, mail order business has become one of the most popular money making opportunities for people who want to own their own business. People are doing it full time or on a part-time basis. According to the estimation on the Internet, for every two seconds, there are 800 mail order businesses coming into existence today which makes mail order one of the fastest growing segments in direct marketing. The driving force behind mail order business rush is the fact that it offers people a great opportunity to make money at the convenience of their home without big financial commitment to get started and the fact that more and more people are doing their shopping needs via mail order delivery.